UNSETTLING
LENT

A DEVOTIONAL

UNSETTLING
LENT

A DEVOTIONAL

Brian Kaylor, Angela Parker,
& Beau Underwood

chalice
PRESS

Cover Design: Kimberly Mayfield/ Kfx Graphic Design

Print: 9780827238640

EPUB: 9780827238657

EPDF: 9780827238664

ChalicePress.com

Printed in the United States of America

Dear Readers,

In the fall of 2021 as Advent neared, the editorial team at *Word&Way* (a Christian media company based in Missouri and founded in 1896) discussed ideas for a possible series related to the impending season. But things didn't quite feel right.

The second COVID year weighed on us with the Delta variant surging (and unknown to us, the Omicron strain would hit hard during Advent). The racial justice protests of the previous year gave way to a growing whitelash as people attacked efforts to combat racism as some sort of "critical race theory" bogeyman. And the year had started with an insurrection at the U.S. Capitol in an attempt to overturn a democratic election.

How do we think about Advent in a time like that? How do we mark that holy season in such unsettling times?

And that's when we realized we need to unsettle Advent. After all, Jesus didn't show up on a silent night in a peaceful land with cute little angels like our domesticated versions of the story too often suggest. Jesus came during a time much like ours. A time of death. A time of racial injustices. A time of insurrection.

So, we launched a pop-up Substack newsletter with a daily devotion emailed each morning to people who signed up. We chose that format since we were already experiencing success with our regular Substack publication, *A Public Witness*, where Beau Underwood and I continue to publish in-depth reports each week on important issues of faith, culture, and politics. (So sign up at publicwitness.wordandway.org.) About twenty writers joined us in helping with this *Unsettling Advent* series that you can still read today at advent.wordandway.org (and that even won an award from the Religion Communicators Council). One writer was Angela Parker, who has also written other pieces for *Word&Way*. Another was Brad Lyons, publisher of Chalice Press. A few months later, over coffee, Beau and I talked with Brad about writing some Lenten devotions. He suggested we need to now unsettle Lent. So, that's exactly what we're doing.

Beau, Angela, and I plotted together over Zoom to bring this book to life. But now it's your turn. We hope these devotionals will enrich your experience over these several weeks as we walk toward the cross and the empty tomb. After the first half-week introducing Lent, each week we'll focus on a new theme: announcing the kingdom, social challenges, crossing boundaries, conspiracies/plotting, social/political context, and then Holy Week.

We hope you'll be challenged to not let the biblical texts hide behind stained-glass windows and cute coloring pages. We hope these devotionals will challenge and even irritate you as you reflect on them. Because they did for us as we put them together. Thanks for joining us on this unsettling adventure during unusual times.

—Brian Kaylor

1. Marked by the Cross

Genesis 3:19
"You are dust, and to dust you shall return."
(Genesis 3:19)

I once spent hours on a street corner confronting random strangers with their mortality. My witness was more subtle than shouting, "You're going to die!" Instead, as they walked by me on a cold spring day, I politely asked them if they wanted to be ritually marked with ashes. It was after they said "yes" that I hit them with the punch while moving my thumb across their forehead: "You are dust, and to dust you shall return."

Like other church pastors, I was participating in a movement called "Ashes to Go" that's designed to take the Christian rituals of Ash Wednesday beyond the walls of church sanctuaries. While meant to make participation more convenient for busy people, the dislocation of the sacred act also adds to its meaning. Scripture's morbid witness disrupts a world in denial about the reality of death.

There's nothing more unsettling than reflecting on the brevity of our existence. Left to our own devices, none of us will make it out alive. So, we place our hope elsewhere. Trusting God with our present days and eternal futures requires us to first get out of the way. Finding the proper orientation requires taking the spotlight off ourselves.

So we start the journey through Lent by marking ourselves with a cross of ashes. A reminder of the death we cannot escape. Turning away from ourselves, we remember that Jesus shares our fate. Now will we let his cross disturb our lives enough to change our world?

Prayer: Holy One, place your mark on us this Lenten season. By admitting we will die, allow us to live with a new hope in the life you offer us in Jesus Christ. Amen.

—Beau Underwood

2. Encountering the Mystery of the Kingdom of God

Mark 4:10-20

"To you have been given the secret of the kingdom of God, but for those outside, everything comes in parables." (Mark 4:11)

Lent is a time of transition from ordinary times to extraordinary times. Such a transition can be wonderful, encouraging, discombobulating, and even mysterious. Entering a season of mystery means that often our hearts and minds experience disquiet because we have no understanding about how the mystery will unfold before us.

As the twelve disciples encircle Jesus, they are at the beginning of a journey that will unfold the mystery of the kingdom of God before them. As we journey together through Lent 2023, please know that there may be moments when the unfolding mystery will be unsettling. Our journey is a movement from ordinary times to extraordinary times, but it is also a movement from personal spirituality to communal moments of speaking truth to power and speaking truth to ourselves in our present political and social situations.

Even as we begin to unsettle Lent in these extraordinary times, may we indeed begin to look, so that we may perceive, understand, and turn again to be forgiven. In this time, we will ask hard questions. Have we ignored the racial battles going on around us? Have we ignored the rise of White Christian Nationalism? Do we place our proverbial heads in the sand because of political and social difficulties? Have we ignored God's call to cross boundaries and have conversations with people vastly different from (yet quite similar to) ourselves? Just as the disciples were confused about the unfolding mystery of the kingdom of God, our hope for this devotional is for you to experience the same unsettling even as you proceed with a greater awareness and newness of service to Christ after these forty-seven days.

Prayer: *May God's mercy and grace be upon us as we begin to delve into the mystery of the kingdom of God and our work in God's movement in the world. Amen.*

—Angela N. Parker

3. What Are You Giving Up?

Acts 14:21-25

"Paul and Barnabas appointed elders for them in each church and, with prayer and fasting, committed them to the Lord, in whom they had put their trust." (Acts 14:23)

Perhaps you've already received the question this year. What are you giving up for Lent?

A 2021 poll by YouGov listed the most common things people said they would give up for Lent that year.[1] Food items topped the list, like desserts, soda, fast food, and alcohol. But also in the top ten were things like social media, watching TV, and video games. Apparently, technology and modern treats make it harder to be holy!

While not in that poll, there's a trend I've also noticed on Facebook (because I don't give up social media for Lent) of people giving up things during Lent that don't quite fit in the chocolate or video game genres. Like single-use plastic for Lent. The Church of England helped popularize that Lenten challenge in 2018. But I wonder if it misses the point.

If we're really concerned about the ways we are choking our oceans with islands of plastic waste and destroying our planet with the carbon footprint necessary to create such plastic, then maybe we should do more than give it up for forty days. I'm convicted by my use of plastic year-round and know I need to improve my care of creation in the 318 days beyond Lent.

Jesus fasted from food in the desert not because it was bad but because it was good. But if we're moving beyond necessities and indulgences to the things destroying us or harming our neighbors, we don't need to just fast more but also sin no more.

Prayer: Creator God, help me to give up what I need during this season to focus more on you and how I need you. And help me to remove from my life all year those things which reap destruction upon this planet and those who live here. Amen.

—Brian Kaylor

---

[1] Linley Sanders, "What are Americans giving up for Lent 2021?," YouGov-America, Feb. 17, 2021, https://today.yougov.com/topics/lifestyle/articles-reports/2021/02/17/what-are-americans-giving-up-lent-2021.

4. We May be Dust, But We Don't Have to Look Dusty!

Matthew 6:16-18

"And whenever you fast, do not look dismal, like the hypocrites."
(Matthew 6:16)

In her book *This Here Flesh,* Cole Arthur Riley writes, "We've grown numb to the idea that we ourselves are made of the dust, mysteriously connected to the goodness of the creation that surrounds us."[2]

Many devotionals highlight the Genesis 3:19 narrative which states, "You were made from dust and from dust you shall return." While that may be very well true, Jesus's sermon reminds me that even though we may look dust, we do not have to be dusty!

Jesus instructs the crowds of people not to be dismal or like the hypocrites when they fast. Personally, I am a lover of makeup. Eyeshadow palettes and lipsticks sometimes make my heart flutter with happiness. So, even in the midst of my fasting, social activism, or seminary teaching, I love to wear a "full face" and a smile no matter what. What face are you presenting to the world? In our justice work, similar to our fasting, we must put our best faces forward so God our Father sees the work without us announcing the work to other people. The point is that we *do the work!* While announcing his ministry through the sermon, Jesus also serves as a model on how to do our work with proper focus. As we embark on "Unsettling Lent," let us all remember that there is work without looking dusty, ashy, unkempt, or worse. Put your best face forward as our unsettling begins.

Prayer: May God's grace be that shining oil anointing our faces as we unsettle Lent and begin to do the justice work and solidarity that God has called this to do. Amen.

—Angela N. Parker

---

[2]Cole Arthur Riley, This Here Flesh (New York: Convergent), 7.

5. Do I Need That Kind of Power?

Luke 4:1-13

"Then the devil led him up and showed him in an instant all the kingdoms of the world." (Luke 4:5)

As a seminary professor, I have to disavow my students of the false idea that politics have no place in the biblical text. Often, students bring the "separation of church and state" into their readings of scripture. Some argue that Jesus was not interested in politics. However, good Christians run the risk of damaging peoples' lives and faith with such a belief.

In Luke's temptation of Jesus, the Tempter offers Jesus "all of the kingdoms of the world" along with the authority attached to them. The Greek word that Luke uses is *oikoumene*. This word connotes the idea of the "administrative unit of the Roman Empire" and differs from a common Greek word *cosmos* that biblical readers recognize from John 3:16.

Luke uses the same word in Luke 2:1 when he writes about Caesar Augustus registering the whole *oikoumene*. Luke specifically places the birth of Jesus in conversation with the Roman emperor. The Devil is essentially saying, "Worship me and I will give you all of the glory of the Roman Empire." He tries to overwhelm Jesus with Empire! How are we overwhelmed by Empire in today's contexts? Beginning in 2016, a whole group of "Christians" became enamored with a former president who promised "power." Such power is antithetical to the gospel of Jesus. So, instead of giving up bread or chocolate for Lent, perhaps we should give up political power in the name of Christianity.

Prayer: *Most Holy God, please disavow me of the desire to gain political power that I can lord over other people. In Jesus's name, amen.*

—Angela N. Parker

6. An Urgent Mission

Luke 4:16-21

"He began by saying to them, 'Today this scripture is fulfilled in your hearing.'" (Luke 4:21)

Procrastination often arises when we face hard decisions or difficult tasks. Few of us relish conflict or struggle, so why rush into it when there's so many convenient distractions on our phones or another episode to stream?

Here's one of those moments when Jesus confronts our worst impulses. In affirmation of Jewish practice, Jesus attends synagogue on the Sabbath and uses scripture to make an announcement about his identity. He prophetically announces his messianic mission. Jesus is anointed to bring good news to the poor, healing to the sick, and freedom to the oppressed.

Not only that, but it's happening "today." Jesus isn't wasting any time. What he speaks aloud will happen because his agenda reflects the desires of God. In the person, teachings, and ministry of Jesus, we starkly see the contrasting priorities between the realm of God and those holding social power in the world.

Unfortunately, few willingly give up power. Turning the world upside down as Jesus promises will prove costly for those benefiting from the status quo. As the theologian Frederick Christian Bauerschmidt notes in *The Love That is God*, "Jesus does not merely die but is killed by powerful forces who take offense at his life."[3]

There's a direct connection between Jesus's proclamation that the kingdom of God has arrived and his eventual crucifixion. Despite the risks, Jesus didn't hesitate to challenge the powers that be with the power of God. Are we equally eager to cause such offense regardless of the costs?

Prayer: O God, may the good news of Jesus found in love, in liberation, in healing, and in justice be heard from our lips and seen from our hands. Do not let us delay in witnessing to the radical ways our world needs to change. As citizens of your kingdom we pray, amen.

—Beau Underwood

---

[3]Frederick Christian Bauerschmidt, *The Love That Is God* (Grand Rapids: Eerdmanns, 2020), 30.

7. The Problem with Home

Luke 4:22-30
"'Truly I tell you,' Jesus continued, 'no prophet is accepted in his hometown.'" (Luke 4:24)

Hometowns can be odd places for those who move away. Places change and people evolve in ways that render the once familiar into something strange. Yet that distance often isn't recognized or respected. Despite all that is different, you can return home and still be treated the same.

After announcing his prophetic mission in the synagogue at Nazareth, Jesus is met with outrage rather than joy. They drove him out of town with the intention to kill him. It's not the initial reaction you'd expect to the news that the reign of God is arriving.

Perhaps expectations got in the way. Nazareth wasn't exactly a highly regarded place (see John 1:46). Jesus didn't fit many traditional Jewish ideas of the Messiah. Plus, these people had watched him grow up. They didn't expect that skinny, awkward carpenter's son to amount to much.

Luke describes how Jesus evades the murderous crowd but doesn't say anything about his emotional response. Did he anticipate that rejection? What kind of sting did it carry?

Lent is a season designed for reflection and growth. You should emerge from it more committed to following Jesus and serving God's ways. Those who know you the best might struggle the most with accepting such a change. It might be difficult to return to the comforts of "home" once you've been made uncomfortable by demands that follow from the justice and love of God.

But that doesn't really matter because you're no longer after their approval. The expectations that count have also changed.

Prayer: O God, you relentlessly call us toward you. During this Lenten season, instill in us the convictions of our ultimate home. Conform our lives to your expectations made known in Jesus Christ. Amen.

—Beau Underwood

8. Wait, Are We Going to Church?

Mark 1:14-15
"The time has come." (Mark 1:15)

Mark told his gospel in a hurry. The word "immediately" pops up over forty times. Other gospel writers offer longer narratives about Jesus starting his ministry, but Mark outlines it in just two verses. John the Baptist is put in prison and Jesus starts his ministry to declare "the time has come" for "the kingdom of God."

Mark reminds me of a protest leader. Someone ready to grab the bullhorn, march into the street, and get things going. Sure, there's planning behind the scenes, but Mark tells the story from the action in the streets. Because that's where he saw the kingdom of God arriving.

A few years ago, I joined some other ministers to support a march by low-income workers pushing for a living wage and Medicaid expansion. After a rally inside the State Capitol, the crowd shouted and marched a couple blocks for a debriefing lunch at a nearby church. A woman leading chants with a bullhorn apparently didn't know the planned location—and was so surprised she blurted out with her finger still on the button, amplifying her words: "Wait, are we going to a church?"

I've thought of that young woman advocating for a better world for her and her daughter. She clearly didn't think highly of churches—and we probably earned that reputation. But after breaking bread that day inside a church, perhaps she now knows some Christians do care about justice, about her well-being. The kingdom of God arrives in moments like that.

Prayer: *O God of justice, may I recognize your call to bring good news to those ignored and even exploited by other rulers. Help me to see your kingdom at work in the streets and join it. Amen.*

—Brian Kaylor

9. Timid No More! The Beginning of Healthy Confrontation

Mark 1:35-39

"And he went throughout Galilee, proclaiming the message in their synagogues and casting out demons." (Mark 1:39)

How many of us avoid confrontation? Do we believe that once we accept Jesus our lives will be confrontation free? I hope many are saying, "Of course not." Just as Jesus embraced confrontation, contemporary Christians must embrace confrontation as well.

Today's devotional showcases the beginning of Jesus's ministry, when he separates from the crowds to a desert place to pray. Simon and the rest "hunted for him." The Greek word *katadioko* is an interesting word known as a "hapax legomenon," meaning it appears only one time in the entire Greek New Testament. One scholar, R.T. France, argued that the word alludes to the disciples being slightly disgruntled that they had to hunt for Jesus.[4] The ministry was beginning to go well. They did not realize confrontation was ahead!

Careful readers of the Markan narrative note the allusion to difficult confrontations ahead. At 1:39, the writer states that Jesus proclaims the message in "their" synagogues. Already Jesus is entering spaces where he may not receive welcome. Confrontation occurs in their synagogues because they are full of religious elites ***and*** unclean spirits.

How do we handle confrontation in our own spaces? Jesus was not free of confrontation, and neither are we. Since the rise of Trumpism and White Christian Nationalism, I would argue that systems of power and oppression have overtaken many "Christian" churches and must be excised from the Christian arena. As we unsettle Lent this season, we must not be timid anymore but ready for confrontation.

Prayer: *Gracious Lord, please forgive me for the moments when I was timid and did not raise my voice against oppression. God, grant me the courage and the strength to no longer be timid in the face of social injustice. Amen.*

—Angela N. Parker

---

[4]R. T. France, *The Gospel of Mark* (Grand Rapid: Eerdmans, 2002), 112

10. All Together But Still Different

Isaiah 2:1-4

". . .all the nations shall stream to it." (Isaiah 2:2)

Isaiah announces a vision of God's kingdom where the new era declares new relationships between God, God's people, and the nations that have been warring against God's people. Isaiah's vision announces a transformed society in which all of us who are different can get along well, even in the midst of our continued differences.

The Hebrew word for nations is *goiim,* while the Greek Septuagint (the Greek translation of the Hebrew Bible) refers to the nations as the *ethne.* I appreciate both of these words because they signify a variety of definitions for the people understood in Isaiah. Hebrew scholars understand *goiim* as the people who constantly warred against the Israelite nation. Conversely, Greek scholars understand *ethne* as people who share kinship, culture, and common traditions. No matter how we understand these various groups of people, the text shows that there are differences between the people even as they stream to the mountain of God to be in God's presence.

As we imagine streaming into God's presence in the new kingdom, I often wonder if we lose our identities, language, cultures, and traditions. While I do not have a definitive answer, I love reading Isaiah's vision with Revelation 7:9 where the author saw a "great multitude that no one could count, from every nation, from all tribes and peoples and languages. . ." Therefore, the question for us is: Can we imagine God's kingdom where we are all together but still different?

Prayer: *May the God of difference allow us to bless diversities in our midst. Amen.*

—Angela N. Parker

11. Thy Kingdom Come

Matthew 20:20-28

"Grant that one of these two sons of mine may sit at your right and the other at your left in your kingdom." (Matthew 20:21)

The wife of thunder didn't understand the kingdom Jesus came to build. And the Sons of Thunder didn't either. None of the disciples did, but this family sparked ill will with political strategizing ahead of the predicted victory.

We also too often misunderstand the kingdom. We're ready to take over Washington, D.C., and sit in the seats of glory. Like the insurrectionists on January 6, 2021, who stormed the Capitol and then searched for places of power. One man sat in the Speaker of the House's seat with his feet victoriously stretched out onto the desk. Another group gathered at the podium of the Senate chamber to declare victory in the name of Jesus. The "QAnon Shaman" (the guy sporting face paint and a furry hat with horns) led the group in a prayer through his bullhorn.

"Thank you, Heavenly Father, for this opportunity to stand up for God-given unalienable rights," he declared while standing to the right of the man at the main spot of senatorial glory. "Thank you for allowing the United States to be reborn."[5]

This quest to conquer the nation while carrying Christian flags and Jesus signs roared with thunder that day. But Jesus wasn't in the mob. His kingdom doesn't come that way.

"When he came into the kingdom wearing a crown and under a sign declaring him "king," there were men at his right and left." But they weren't sitting on thrones or celebrating in the halls of power. They hung there on crosses beside him.

Prayer: King Jesus, forgive me when I confuse your kingdom with a partisan one seeking temporal power and glory. Cleanse me of my pride and vanity as I seek honors and praise I don't need or deserve. Humble me to daily pick up my cross and follow you.

—Brian Kaylor

---

[5]Brian Kaylor & Beau Underwood, "The prayers of January 6," *A Public Witness*, Jan. 6, 2022, https://publicwitness.wordandway.org/p/the-prayers-of-january-6

12. A Lent Like No Other

Matthew 12:1-8

"If you have known what these words mean, 'I desire mercy, not sacrifice,' you would not have condemned the innocent." (Matthew 12:7)

The most memorable Lenten season for me will long be that of 2020. As the world shut down amid a mysterious and deadly virus, churches quickly found themselves empty during the holiest season of the year. Yet worship didn't stop.

While I celebrate the life-saving vaccines and the drops in death tolls, I also hope we don't just rush back to the old normal. In times of crisis, we might just be forced to learn lessons about worshiping God that we'd otherwise miss in our comfort. Like David and his companions eating the consecrated bread—and then being sainted by Jesus for that seemingly sacrilegious deed.

A moment I'll cherish for years and beyond is Palm Sunday in 2020. By that point, we were a few weeks into virtual worship, which honestly hadn't been that meaningful for us yet. But that Sunday was different.

Finding Sunday School craft ideas online, I helped my eight-year-old son make some palm leaves out of green construction paper, a metal hanger, and tape. As the service burst onto the screen, he ran to grab his winter coat and toss it on the floor. Then he stood on the coat in his Batman pajamas, waving his palm leaves and singing along with the recorded musicians.

At moments during the pandemic as I grew weary and frustrated, even wondering where God was, that picture came back to mind. May our experiences with God in these unique times this Lent similarly carry us through the year.

Prayer: *Sustainer God, help me as I seek you wherever I find myself today. Disrupt my comfort, shake my contentment, confound my wisdom, and silence my arrogance. May this be a season of seeing and worshiping you in new and holy ways.*

—Brian Kaylor

13. Keep Your Hands (and your Legislation) to Yourself!

1 Corinthians 7:1-7

"Now concerning the matters about which you wrote: 'It is well for a man not to touch a woman.'" (1 Corinthians 7:1)

Women face a multitude of social challenges in the twenty-first century. First Corinthians is one of the epistles that engages women's challenges in an interesting way. As a womanist New Testament scholar, part of my job is to read the biblical text with attention to the unique lived experiences of African American women. How can today's focus text enable new ways of engaging and practicing social advocacy during Lent?

When traditional scholars interpret 1 Corinthians 7:1, most do so from a White and masculine viewpoint. However, feminist scholars argue that women were telling men not to touch them. Why would a woman not want to be touched?

Scholars compellingly argue that first century women, after experiencing the indwelling of the Holy Spirit, did not want to submit their bodies to pregnancy since first century women died at particularly high rates during childbirth. Similarly, in today's contemporary context, Black women suffer high maternal mortality rates. Moreover, since the overturning of *Roe v. Wade*, maternal health experts argue poor Black and Brown women will have less access to abortion care and thus fall into deeper levels of poverty. What is the role of Christians in a post-*Roe* world for women facing difficult challenges during pregnancy? Only time will tell.

Prayer: *To the Most-High God who also looks low, please provide courage and gumption to those desiring to ease the challenges of impoverished women and children around the world. May we show up in ways that are tangible and life giving to our disadvantaged siblings. In Jesus's name, Amen.*

—Angela N. Parker

14. The Poor Among Us

Matthew 26:6-13

"For you always have the poor with you, but you will not always have me." (Matthew 26:11)

I spent several years working on anti-poverty issues in Washington, D.C. My days were spent in meetings on Capitol Hill and at the White House, while my evenings often included a run around the nation's capital.

Discussing anti-poverty policy is an abstract exercise. Jogging around downtown D.C., where unhoused residents of the city slept on the sidewalks as powerful people walked right by, made the issue far more concrete.

In too many conversations, Christians will reference this biblical passage in defending the status quo. In their thinking, even Jesus acknowledges poverty is intractable and our efforts to address it are futile. Conveniently, this mindset justifies the inequities of our society. Jesus seems to let those who have more off the hook for not helping those with much less.

That's not the lesson Jesus intended his followers to learn. The expensive oil was not wasted. As the theologian Stanley Hauerwas noted, "This woman poured precious ointment on a poor person. The poor that we will always have with us is Jesus. It is to the poor that all extravagance is to be given."[6]

The enduring presence of poverty is a call to action, not resignation. Following the moral example of the woman who anoints Jesus, our resources should not be selfishly kept for our own devices. That would be the real waste. Instead, they should be extravagantly used to bless the poor and vulnerable among us. After all, in them we see the face of Jesus.

Prayer: Beautiful One, our material and spiritual poverty is a dangerous mix. We offer righteous-sounding justifications for ignoring the physical needs of others. Reorient our priorities to become more like the woman who anointed Jesus so that we might also become a blessing to the poor and forgive us for the sins of our neglect. In Christ's name we pray, amen.

—Beau Underwood

---

[6]Stanley Hauerwas, *Matthew* (Grand Rapids: Brazos Press, 2006), 215.

15. A Strange Land

Matthew 25:31-36

"I was a stranger and you invited me in." (Matthew 25:35)

I realized our political polarization had crept into the church following a sermon on immigration. Earlier in my tenure, I preached about refugee resettlement as a witness to Christian unity. It was one of the few common efforts undertaken by U.S. Catholics, evangelicals, and mainline Protestants. Nobody objected to that message.

A different response arose many years later when I critiqued the harsh immigration policies of the Trump Administration, specifically the practice of detaining migrant children in chain-link cages. Conversations followed with church members about the inappropriateness of politics coming from the pulpit.

That pushback reminded me of a meeting I participated in with a group of Christian immigration advocates and an influential senator in Washington, D.C. During a debate over the DREAM Act, which tried to shield from deportation undocumented immigrants who came to the U.S. as children, another senator approached him and said, "I'm praying for you on this. I can't vote with you. The politics at home are too tough, but I'm praying for you."

The senator was flabbergasted by the cowardice of this response. He expressed frustration and resignation about the ability of Congress to tackle immigration policy in a humane way.

"Senator," I dared to say, "you should remind your colleague that sometimes God asks us to be the answer to our own prayers."

We plead with God to draw us closer to Jesus. That's not going to happen until we realize he's with the strangers we demonize and fear.

Prayer: God, your people were once strangers in a foreign land. Forgetting that part of our story, we reject and oppress the strangers among us. Unharden our hearts, that we might become more welcoming of immigrants and, by doing so, become more welcoming of Jesus. We pray this in his precious name, amen.

—Beau Underwood

16. Jesus and Mass Incarceration

Matthew 4:12-17

"Now when Jesus heard that John had been arrested, he withdrew to Galilee." (Matthew 4:12)

Communities of color face high rates of mass incarceration. What does it mean to consider the early Jesus community as a community of color in the time of the Roman Empire? I do not think the consideration is such a leap since John the Baptist was arrested and executed by Roman imperial forces. Accordingly, anyone associated with John would be labeled as a possible criminal as well. Since Jesus was baptized by John the Baptist, it is not difficult to imagine the Empire labeling Jesus as "criminal" since he begins his ministry with similar language to John the Baptist when he states, "Repent, for the kingdom of God has come near."

Writer Michelle Alexander discusses labels that are placed on inmates as a result of being incarcerated. Alexander highlights how Black and Brown men were incarcerated as a result of the war on drugs.[7] However, when drug infestation moves into predominantly White neighborhoods, the language of the war on drugs changes to treat drug abuse as a medical issue. Black and Brown drug abusers were labeled as "criminal" while White users needed medical attention.

How does this labeling affect our reading of scripture? Just as Jesus was already labeled criminal and troublemaker, contemporary readers must read scripture with a sympathetic view toward contemporary incarceration. What would it look like if the church today specifically aligned herself with Black and Brown "criminals" in the age of the New Jim Crow?

Prayer: *Gracious God, please forgive us for turning a blind eye to the issues of mass incarceration. May we work to create a national movement that corrects the wrongs of the new Jim Crow system. Amen.*

—Angela N. Parker

---

[7]Michelle Alexander, *The New Jim Crow* (New York: New Press, 2012).

17. Behind Bars

Hebrews 13:1-3
"Remember those who are in prison, as though you were in prison with them." (Hebrews 13:3)

At the end of my first pastoral visit inside a maximum security prison, I asked my incarcerated conversation partner an unintentionally stupid question: "So, what happens now?" I wasn't sure about the protocols, but he didn't miss the opportunity to crack a joke.

"Well, I stay in here, and you go out there."

He flashed a grin and then explained the process to me. While I appreciated his sense of humor, I found the experience surreal. I largely had control over my life. He had almost no control over his.

Another inmate I visit has been wrongfully incarcerated for decades. Beyond his own protestation, the prosecutor's office and political leaders acknowledge his innocence, but there's a legal and bureaucratic tussle over how to free him. While that sorts itself out, he unjustly remains in prison.

Imagine if those in power put themselves in his shoes. Instead of throwing up roadblocks or remaining passive, seeing themselves "in prison with [him]" would cause them to act with great haste.

Our prison system is designed to help us forget. By removing offenders from society (sometimes necessarily so), we gain an assurance of safety and lose our sense of obligation towards the incarcerated.

That attitude puts us at odds with Jesus, who provocatively says that visiting prisoners is an encounter with him (Matthew 25:41-45). When it comes to those in prison, the book of Hebrews demands our empathy rather than our obliviousness. We have to go there if we want to fully meet Jesus.

Prayer: *Ignoring the least among us is easy to do, especially when they are locked away. Yet, O God, you expect solidarity with our incarcerated brothers and sisters from us. May our remembering them provoke reflection on what true justice in our society might look like. Help us to realize that vision in the name of our liberating savior. Amen.*

—Beau Underwood

18. Beating Guns

Micah 4:1-5

"They will beat their swords into plowshares
and their spears into pruning hooks.
Nation will not take up sword against nation,
nor will they train for war anymore." (Micah 4:3)

During Lent of 2019, I worshiped one night by hammering hot steel on a blacksmith's anvil. That orange metal taking the blows had been a gun. Soon, it would be a garden spade.

If Micah showed up today, he might look something like my friend Mike Martin, a bearded Mennonite blacksmith. Mike and his ministry RAWtools have been beating guns into garden tools for over a decade. On another occasion, I joined Mike and his father as they disarmed 150 guns to beat and reform. As I used a power saw to slice through a deadly idol, fiery sparks lit up the parking lot, and smoke filled the air like incense. This was our offering to God.

Some days when gun violence fills the news, I feel hopeless. But prophets like Micah and Mike show us another world is possible. When you live in a time where there is injustice, when you live in a time where there is violence, when you live in a time where the blood is crying out from the ground, and when you live in a time where—despite all of that—those in power say the status quo is okay, that's when the prophets show up.

We do not have to accept that the world is the way it should be or must be. So, when politicians say that "thoughts and prayers" are all that we can offer amid an epidemic of gun violence, I say I know that's not true. For I've smelled the smoke and seen the fire.

Prayer: God of the nations, teach people how to walk in your ways. Help us as a society to transform our weapons of war into tools that bring sustenance and life. And help me to be a peacemaker in my community.

—Brian Kaylor

19. Conquered

John 16:31-33

"In the world you face persecution, but take courage: I have conquered the world!" (John 16:33)

Many Christians "bury the alleluia" during Lent. Silence replaces the shouts of praise in recognition of the solemn season. Like giving up an indulgence or fasting, this verbal self-denial is another way of preparing individual and collective spirits for walking with Jesus to the cross. The tortuous, gory destination demands subdued language.

The chaos, carnage, and challenges of our world can also make it difficult to utter the word *alleluia*. Praising God is easy in joyful times. But when illness arrives or a mass shooting occurs or racism rears its hideous head yet again, our tongues understandably fall silent. What thanks or praise can be offered then?

In his life and teachings, Jesus did not celebrate the world as it is but testified to how things should be. He invited people to join in the reign of God that condemned the structural sins plaguing society and the hardness disfiguring human hearts. Seeking such transformation brought opposition then, just as the work of pursuing social justice does now.

Sundays in Lent are not counted as part of the season's forty days. They are often referred to as "Little Easters," where the power of resurrection is proclaimed even as the march towards the cross continues on. In these moments of reprieve, Christians who bury their alleluias will often allow their praises to rise again.

It's a good practice in our daily lives too. We find the courage to keep praising God even when beaten down because, despite appearances, Jesus has conquered the world.

Prayer: *Resurrecting God, on this "Little Easter," may our hearts be filled with praise. We glorify you not because of how things are now but because of how you promise things will eventually be. Help us overcome our resistance to that transformation, so that we might participate in Jesus's overcoming the world. Amen.*

—Beau Underwood

20. The Spikes

Luke 5:12-16

"Jesus reached out his hand and touched the man." (Luke 5:13)

Our cities are increasingly hostile. Not the people, the architecture. A specialty of urban design called "hostile architecture" experiments with keeping people without homes from hanging out in public spaces. Like installing fences to block off areas under stairwells where people would find cover while sleeping. Or altering benches so that people could sit but not lie down—like adding metal pipes to divide up seating spots or titling them so you would roll off if you lie down. Or, most inhumanely, installing spikes on ledges, under overpasses, or other places where people are likely to sleep or even just sit and rest.

We've spent our money crafting spikes so that unhoused persons would have no place to even lay their heads. Each of these "solutions" involves spending thousands of dollars to "fix" one spot. Rather than investing in helping people, we shove them farther to the margins.

Jesus instead reaches out and touches the lepers. As does Lindsey Krinks, a street chaplain in Nashville, Tennessee, who ministers with unhoused persons. She wrote in her book *Praying with Our Feet* about spending Holy Week in the streets reading the biblical accounts. Like reading about Jesus's kingdom outside city hall, reading about multiplying the loaves and fishes under a bridge, and celebrating the Last Supper in a park with grape juice they bought from panhandling and crusty rolls they found dumpster diving.

If we're looking for Jesus, we need to go into the streets. We'll probably find him harassed by fences and spikes.

Prayer: *Gracious God, help me to have compassion for those you offer compassion. Help me to see you in the streets today. May I find ways to be part of the healing solutions for those my community pushes aside.*

—Brian Kaylor

21. The Bible in Real Life

John 15:12-17

"No one has greater love than this, to lay down one's life for one's friends." (John 15:13)

The truth proclaimed by the Bible is everywhere, if only we are willing to see it. Of course, that qualification is a big one. There are lots of times when we aren't capable of seeing what Jesus demands of us or, worse yet, we recognize it but refuse to follow. So, when people embody God's message, we take notice.

In 2014, my attention was captured by news reports about a group of young men in Sierra Leone. Referred to as the "burial boys," they dug graves for deceased community members who died during the Ebola epidemic.

Not only was the job hard, but it was hazardous and thankless. They risked exposure to the virus and faced ostracism from their own family and friends. They were willing to give up their physical and social lives for the sake of others.

Obviously, I have no clue if they were followers of Jesus, but those courageous young men taught me—and hopefully other Christians—what the words of John's gospel meant. They demonstrated that the deepest form of love is more costly than sentimental. It compels us to go where we'd rather not.

Jesus demonstrates this throughout his public ministry when he dines with sinners, touches those deemed "unclean," and transgresses other social boundaries. He never lets rules get in the way of love. And he loves the way he does because none of us are strangers to him. He calls us all friends. That's quite a statement.

Prayer: Loving God, knowing that Jesus calls us friend, may we trust your love even more and cross whatever boundaries love requires of us. As followers of Jesus, we pray, amen.

—Beau Underwood

22. Looking in the Face of the Other

Matthew 15:21-28
"I was sent only to the lost sheep of the house of Israel."
(Matthew 15:24)

The story of the Canaanite woman of Matthew 15:21-28 is an interesting story of crossing boundaries. As Jesus has left his own comfort zone within a Jewish district, he crosses over into Gentile towns known as Tyre and Sidon. Just then, a Canaanite woman begins screaming after Jesus. How are we to understand Jesus's refusal to speak with her at first?

The standard Calvinistic response is to argue that Jesus builds her faith by not responding immediately to her request. However, I think there is more to the story. Even though Jesus specifically states that he has only come to the lost sheep of the house of Israel, we know that Matthew 8:5 records the story of Jesus healing the servant of a Roman Centurion, so there is more to his encounter with the Canaanite woman.

Reading the Canaanite woman with the genealogy of Matthew 1, scholars note that there are Canaanite women named in the genealogy. Not only is naming women in a genealogy uncommon, but the gospel writer names sexually suspect Canaanite women like Tamar and Rahab instead of the accepted matriarchs like Sarah, Leah, and Rachel. Is Jesus looking at the face of the other and seeing himself and his foremothers in the process? Are there moments when we must look in the face of the other and see ourselves?

Prayer: *To the God who builds bridges, please forgive us for not recognizing ourselves in the face of the other. Please provide opportunities for us to commune with the other in our midst. Amen.*

—Angela N. Parker

23. The Good Parable

Luke 10:25-37
*"'Which of these three do you think was a neighbor to the man who
fell into the hands of robbers?'
The expert in the law replied, 'The one who had mercy on him.'
Jesus told him, 'Go and do likewise.'" (Luke 10:36-37)*

Your Bible likely ruins this story. Some editor thought they'd help by adding subtitles. So, they called this section something like "the Parable of the Good Samaritan." What a horrible way to treat a good story! It'd be like if a production company had released M. Night Shyamalan's *The Sixth Sense* with (spoiler alert) the title *He's Dead the Whole Time*.

When Jesus started his story, no one in his audience expected a Samaritan as the hero. More likely, after Jesus mentioned a man getting robbed, somebody mumbled, "I bet it was those damned Samaritans." The plot twist so surprised the seminary professor whose question sparked the story that the man couldn't bring himself to say, "The Samaritan."

Clarence Jordan captured this dynamic brilliantly in *The Cotton Patch Gospel* translation that places Jesus in Georgia in the mid-twentieth century. After a White preacher and White music leader sped by on that road between Atlanta and Albany, a Black man stopped. But the Sunday School teacher caught himself as he responded to Jesus's question, "Why, of course, the nigg—I mean, er... well, er... the one who treated me kindly."

That's the shock we need today as our politicians demonize the "other." Perhaps today Jesus would spin a tale about a far-right, Christian Nationalist, anti-refugee politician being helped by a gay Syrian refugee. Or perhaps it would be a saga where the hero at the end wears a transgender flag T-shirt. Or a red MAGA hat. Jesus, stop meddling.

Prayer: *Merciful God, help me to see others as my neighbors. May I serve those I distrust, love those I fear. Rather than always centering myself as the hero of the story, shock me afresh with your unlimiting, unrelenting love.*

—Brian Kaylor

24. Us vs. Them

John 4:1-26

"The Samaritan woman said to Jesus, 'How is it that you, a Jew, ask a drink of me, a woman of Samaria?' (Jews do not share things in common with Samaritans)" (John 4:9)

The ideology of Christian Nationalism operates by drawing boundaries. Conservative White Christians (and those who share their views) enjoy a privileged status in society because they are the rightful heirs of this "Christian nation."

They are the insiders who deserve to wield power because they define and defend "American" values. Those operating by different beliefs and understandings are illegitimate outsiders, neither fully American nor truly Christian. At the extreme, violence by the insiders is justified to defeat and oppress the outsiders because it protects the social order.

Among the many biblical passages that are difficult to square with Christian Nationalism is this passage from John 4. A socially-ostracized woman visits the community well at noon, which is the hottest part of the day and means others won't be around. There she unexpectedly encounters the Messiah, who violates cultural taboos around gender and religion in approaching her. Jewish men did not strike up conversations with the Samaritan women.

Throughout the gospels, Jesus regularly transgresses the boundaries of society. Our demarcations clearly labeling some people as "in" and other people as "out" serve human ends of preserving power and privilege. They regularly get in the way of people drawing close to God.

Christian Nationalism demands loyalty to the distinctions it draws. It wants you to become part of the "us" that sees you fighting against "them." In contrast, Jesus asks that you trust him enough to cross those boundaries in witness to the radical love of God.

Prayer: *Transcendent One, allow us to escape the boxes we put you and others in. This Lenten season, may we hear anew all the things Jesus proclaims to us in spirit and in truth. Amen.*

—Beau Underwood

25. Crossing From Certainty to Uncertainty

Philippians 1:12-18

"These proclaim Christ out of love, knowing that I have been put here for the defense of the gospel; the others proclaim Christ out of selfish ambition, not sincerely but intending to increase my suffering in my imprisonment." (Philippians 1:16-17)

Scholars of Philippians highlight the joy that exudes in this letter even though Paul is an imprisoned person. There is a sense of confidence in vocation to spread the gospel of Christ. However, what is most striking about today's particular passage is Paul's joy even when he recognizes that some proclaim Christ from envy and rivalry or out of selfish ambition. Paul's only concern is that Christ is proclaimed.

Pondering Paul's joy makes me ask, "How do I proclaim Christ today?" Do I proclaim Christ with a "know-it-all" certainty that makes others think I have all the "right" answers? Truthfully, I have always understood the Christian apologetic movement to exude such confidence. How special for them. (Yes, please read sarcasm in this comment.) As I ponder my own Christian journey, I appreciate Paul's language in 1:16, where he talks about an apology or defense of the gospel.[8] What I now realize is that my defense of the gospel is not a defense of the certainty of the gospel but is actually a defense against certainty. In my walk with Christ, I have been blessed to witness to more souls based on my stance of uncertainty versus a certainty stance. That has been one of my biggest selling points for Jesus. I may not be "certain" about everything, and, to be honest, friends, I am OK with that. How about you?

Prayer: *Precious Lord, please forgive me for the times where I exhibited certainty. God, allow me to be content with the mystery of Jesus, the mystery of the Bible, and the mystery of your Spirit doing something different day after day. In Jesus's name, amen.*

—Angela N. Parker

---

[8]David Pickering. "Chesterton, Apologetics, and the Art of Positioning." *Journal of Inklings Studies* 10, no. 1 (2020): 37–51. https://doi.org/10.3366/ink.2020.0061.

26. Musing Against the Replacement Conspiracy Theory

Esther 9:24-28

"Haman son of Hammedatha the Agagite, the enemy of all the Jews, had plotted against the Jews to destroy them, and had cast Pur— that is 'the lot'—to crush and destroy them" (Esther 9:24).

I think that one of the most surreal moments I have experienced in the past few years has been watching the march in Charlottesville, Virginia, where some chanted, "The Jews will not replace us." The replacement conspiracy theory has been a talking point in many far-right websites in the past few years. Have Christian nationalists not critically thought about Supersessionism as it relates to claiming that Christianity is better than Judaism and that the United States is a Christian nation that is exceptionally better than other nations?

Turning to the book of Esther, I ponder some of these questions since it highlights conspiracy, nationalism, and sexism. The book details Esther's elevation to the station of queen after the king had one-night stands with women from all corners of the kingdom. The previous queen, Vashti, had been deposed since she would not appear nude before her husband and his drunken friends. Queen Esther saves the Jewish nation from Haman's conspiracy, thus allowing various religious and ethnic identities to live in Babylon for a peaceful time period.

If Christians desire to be a "Christian" nation, we would not conspire against God's original chosen people. Conspiracy is not a valid position to aspire to. We must aspire to live in an interreligious society where Christians, Jews, Muslims, Buddhists, etc. all live and have a right to enjoy religious freedom. I do not know if any of this is possible, but it should be every Christian's aspiration.

Prayer: Gracious God, we have been enamored with the privileges bestowed upon us through White supremacy. Please stop us from idealizing a fusion of Christianity with American civic life that assumes White supremacy and patriarchy.

—Angela N. Parker

27. Whitewashed Monuments

Matthew 23:29-32

*"Woe to you, teachers of the law and Pharisees, you hypocrites!
You build tombs for the prophets and decorate the graves of the
righteous." (Matthew 23:29)*

When Martin Luther King Jr. Day rolls around, tweets emerge from people clearly missing the point.[9] Like politicians demonizing anti-racism efforts but then tweeting the only line they apparently know from King about judging people by their character. Or like the NFL—that blacklisted Colin Kaepernick for peaceful protest—having the gall to tweet they celebrated King's "life, legacy, and lasting impact."

Or like the U.S. Marines tweeting praise for him as "a man whose fight for equality strengthened our nation," before adding a quote from King: "A man who won't die for something is not fit to live." Of course, the Marines must've missed King's prophetic critique of militarism. For instance, King thundered at Riverside Church in New York City, "A nation that continues year after year to spend more money on military defense than on programs of social uplift is approaching spiritual death." (Feel free to tweet that!)

Or like the NRA that tweeted they "honor the profound life and legacy" of King, adding he needed a gun for his "right to self-defense." God, they truly don't get it!

Our nation built a gorgeous monument to King on the National Mall but continues to fight his life's work (just like we did when he was alive). Voting rights are under attack. Income inequality soars, thanks to capitalistic greed. Military spending triumphs over basic health care or affordable housing. We build tombs for the prophets our ancestors killed while we attack the next generation of prophets.

Prayer: God of history, illuminate the blind spots in my understanding of the past. Help me to not repeat the pattern of condemning the prophets today even while priding myself in praising those of the past. May I be a voice for justice and peace in this time.

—Brian Kaylor

---

[9] See these and other tweets compiled by Sophie Weiner, "Who did the worst MLK Day tweet?," *Splinter News,* Jan. 21, 2019, https://splinternews.com/who-did-the-worst-mlk-day-tweet-1831937329

28. Jesus and QAnon

Luke 8:16-18

"For there is nothing hidden that will not be disclosed, and nothing concealed that will not be known or brought out into the open."
(Luke 8:17)

The ideas were both unbelievable and familiar. A fellow Christian explained to me how the "deep state" was in control, but soon the truth would be revealed and justice served. Without explicitly professing adherence to QAnon, his words conveyed his loyalties.

Of course, none of the speculations came to fruition, but that didn't change his thinking. When politics or culture heads in directions we dislike, the world feels beyond our control. Conspiracy theories offer comfort and hope. The Internet makes them accessible while connecting us to others who normalize our suspicions.

John's gospel promises that "the truth will make [us] free" (8:32), but polling indicates many Christians are captivated by conspiratorial ideas. This shouldn't surprise us. After all, Jesus was constantly teaching in parables. The truth of his teaching remained hidden to those without eyes to see and ears to hear. Is there much difference between the parables of the gospel and the conspiracies roiling our society today?

Let me respond with an emphatic yes. Conspiracy theories indulge our confirmation bias. We perceive them as validating and bolstering the views we already hold, especially those out of favor or at odds with reality.

Rather than confirming our suspicions, Jesus's parables challenge us to become different. They teach us alternative ways that upend human conventions and align us with God. Like conspiracy theories, the teachings of Jesus require a leap of faith. But they are self-denying, rather than self-serving. And, once Holy Week arrives, we'll see how they come true.

Prayer: *God of truth, as participants in your divine conspiracy, allow us to reject what is false and hold fast to what is true. Shield us from those peddling self-serving ideas that indulge the worst of human nature. Fill us with edifying words that mold us in your ways. In the name of our teacher, Jesus, we pray, amen.*

—Beau Underwood

29. Not All Counsel is Good Counsel

Matthew 12:9-14

"But the Pharisees went out and conspired against him, how to destroy him." (Matthew 12:14)

As I think about the world since the beginning of the COVID-19 pandemic, it seems to me that our world needs healing from the multiple pandemics of COVID-19, the rise of White Christian Nationalism, racial injustice, and the turbulent economic woes that many are currently facing in our nation. Wouldn't the world be ecstatic if a real, full-bodied Brown Jesus entered into our world and began healing all the sicknesses that we are experiencing today? Not everyone was happy when Jesus began healing in their synagogues. After healing the man with the withered hand, the gospel writer notes that the Pharisees went out and conspired with one another. The Greek author uses the phrase *sumboulion elabon*, signifying the idea of "taking counsel" with one another. The Pharisees were upset that Jesus had healed on the Sabbath and seemingly did not care that Jesus restored a man's hand!

Pondering this text, I cannot help but think of a parallel connection with vaccine reluctance in the age of COVID-19. I still mourn family and friends who died from COVID-19 before vaccines were available. I am also fearful for family members who still refuse the vaccine. Did they receive counsel from trusted physicians or counsel from discredited news sources? We must realize that not all counsel is good counsel and that receiving bad counsel often conspires against our own well-being.

Prayer: *Dear Jesus, we know and accept you as the great physician. Please forgive us when we sought counsel that is contradictory to you. Please point us in the right direction of sound counsel all of the days of our lives. Amen.*

—Angela N. Parker

30. Caesar's Trap

Matthew 22:15-22

"Give therefore to Caesar the things that are Caesar's and to God the things that are God's." (Matthew 25:21)

Michael Flynn, who briefly served as President Trump's first national security advisor and later received a pardon for lying to the FBI, is no stranger to controversy. Still, the trouble he stirred up in late 2021 was noticeably different because it was theological in nature.

"If we are going to have one nation under God, which we must, we have to have one religion," Flynn preached. "One nation under God and one religion under God."[10]

Was he endorsing forced conversion? Was he implying only Christians could live in the United States? The authoritarian logic was both troubling and difficult to unpack. Yet, he clearly saw his version of (the Christian) religion as central to national identity. Religion needed to serve the state. That's quite a contrast with what we find in Matthew's gospel.

Jesus's opponents laid a trap for him. If he endorsed paying taxes to the empire and its false gods, that would compromise his claim to be the Messiah. On the other hand, speaking against the empire would be seditious and bring a heap of trouble. He cleverly escapes by putting Caesar in his place. The empire can keep its graven images, which are no match for the power and magnificence of the invisible God.

Like Michael Flynn, many of us make God too small. We render to Caesar the loyalty that properly belongs to God. Until we fix that fundamental error, our faith is in something less than the transcendent One.

Prayer: *Rescue us, O God, from our paltry visions and partisan projects. Recognizing that all empires will pass away, render us fiercely loyal to your name that is above all names. With Jesus we pray, amen.*

—Beau Underwood

---

[10]Brian Kaylor & Beau Underwood, "One Nation Under Michael Flynn's God," *A Public Witness,* November 16, 2021, https://publicwitness.wordandway.org/p/one-nation-under-michael-flynns-god

31. Cowardly Arrest

Matthew 26:1-4
"They schemed to arrest Jesus secretly and kill him. "But not during the festival," they said, "or there may be a riot among the people." (Matthew 26:3-4)

Several years ago, twenty-three ministers started shouting during a session of the Missouri Senate. Lawmakers refused to expand Medicaid under the Affordable Care Act, leaving a couple hundred thousand people without coverage even as they worked hard in low-income jobs.

So, with the senators at ease on the floor beneath them, clergy started shouting from the gallery to expand Medicaid and "do justice." After several minutes, police tapped on their shoulders, and the ministers peacefully left. Back in the hallways, they joined hundreds of other protesters.

After being briefly processed by police, the ministers expected that to be the end of the matter since charges for peaceful demonstrations at the Capitol are usually dropped. But after the crowd left and the lawmakers went home without expanding Medicaid, a local prosecutor decided to take the "Medicaid 23" to court and seek jail time. In a mass trial, he managed to convict them of trespassing (in a public building) but failed on the charge of obstructing a government function as lawmakers in both parties backed the clergy. They got off with a minor fine.

The cowardly effort to prosecute the clergy after the crowd left reminds me of the treatment of Jesus. Officials would arrest Jesus at night and give him a sham trial. But justice is not so easily stopped. Missouri's governor pardoned all of the clergy who wanted it. And the voters in the state later overruled lawmakers to expand Medicaid (and booted the local prosecutor from office).

Prayer: God of justice, may my voice, my life be given for those who are ignored and oppressed. Help me to bring light on the deeds done in darkness.

—Brian Kaylor

32. Death Grip of Rulers

John 12:1-10
"The chief priests made plans to kill Lazarus as well, for on account of him many of the Jews were going over to Jesus and believing in him." (John 12:10)

When leaders with authoritarian tendencies feel their power slipping away, they create a more dangerous world. King Herod, who slaughtered babies in Bethlehem as a childish plot to prevent a prophesied new king, even killed some of his own sons and his favorite wife amid paranoid fits of fury. Abimelek, in Judges 9, rained death around him as his reign fell apart. And Adolf Hitler, perhaps feeling impotent as Allied forces closed in, executed many of his opponents, like theologian Dietrich Bonhoeffer.

Explaining violent whims of crazed rulers often proves futile. Some kill close advisors, whose real crimes were remaining loyal through it all. Others slaughter innocent civilians as a bloody "Hail Mary" to stall the inevitable. As their glory dims, their inner weakness shines.

On January 6, 2021, we saw the potential of such maddening thirst for power. With a failed and defeated leader cheering his violent mob, cries of, "Hang Mike Pence" rang out, and people constructed gallows outside the Capitol. Even if they killed the vice president, it wouldn't change the fact that Joe Biden won. But the mind of an angry mob rarely aligns with reality.

Similarly, we see the desperation of Jesus's opponents as they plotted to kill not only him but Lazarus, a man whose only "crime" was being alive. Killing a man who died and came back to life seems laughable. But this plotting signaled growing desperation. The corrupting siren call of power blinds us, tempts us to double down instead of repent.

Prayer: *Omnipotent God, help me to trust in you instead of the principalities and powers of this world. May my life be a holy irritant to those who abuse power and devour the innocent. And help me when partisan loyalty tempts me to call evil "good" and good "evil."*

—Brian Kaylor

33. Narrow is the Way

Matthew 7:13-21

"Not everyone who says to me, 'Lord, Lord,' will enter the kingdom of heaven, but only the one who does the will of my Father in heaven." (Matthew 7:21)

The host pastor leaned over to me and lamentably whispered, "This is the most ironic thing I've ever experienced in church." After carefully planning a July Fourth worship service emphasizing how American churches often turn our nation into an idol, it turned out the music director had selected a medley of patriotic hymns for the postlude.

While providing a chuckle, that moment also reminded us that even so-called progressive churches struggle with getting the basics of the gospel right. In this section from Matthew, Jesus makes clear that he wants more than just our profession of faith. Those truly wanting to be his disciples must walk the walk, not just talk the talk.

Proclaiming Jesus to be Lord is a test of loyalty. For the earliest Christians, it was a challenge to the Roman Empire's declaration that Caesar was Lord. Today, it is an enduring question of what gets our ultimate allegiance. If we're honest with ourselves, we often fail this test. From political affiliations to preferences over worship styles, a lot of things get in the way of us following Jesus.

Increasingly, I'm aware how even fights over church doctrines fall into this category. There's a lot of Christians so committed to the "right" beliefs that they get their ethics all wrong. Determined to win an argument, they end up turning people away from Jesus.

Jesus wants us to testify that he is Lord, but he's quite clear that actions speak louder than words.

Prayer: In word and deed, O God, we seek to confess that Jesus is Lord. May the witness of our hands and feet affirm, rather than contradict, what pours out of our mouth. Amen.

—Beau Underwood

34. Augustus, Trumpism, and the Gospel

Luke 2:1-7

"In those days Caesar Augustus issued a decree that a census should be taken of the entire Roman world. (This was the first census that took place while[a] Quirinius was governor of Syria.)" (Luke 2:1-2)

While I know that we are not discussing Advent in this Lenten season, Luke's birth narrative is a great way to explain the social and political contexts in which the gospel occurs. Luke 2:1-7 opens with a decree ordered by Emperor Augustus declaring that all the world should be registered. Luke's writing of Augustus's decree is important politically and socially since Augustus was not only the first emperor of Rome but was also the first emperor connected to the Greek idea of *euangelion*—i.e., the beginning of the gospel.

Original auditors of Luke's gospel would have recognized the innuendo (and danger) of connecting Jesus to the term *euangelion*. Luke's audience lived under the rule of Augustus and would have recognized that the upper echelon of Roman society extracts money from the lower classes in order to line their own coffers. Luke provides great political, social, and economic information in these first few verses of chapter 2.

Thinking through this text, should we consider Caesar Augustus of Luke 2:1-2 as a shining example of political power and someone to emulate? I would argue a definitive no. As we walk this Lenten journey, let us review our relationship with political figures so we are not moved to cheap discipleship of those other than Jesus.

Prayer: *Gracious God, Trumpism still exists in the United States. Please allow a renewed and revitalized relationship with you so that we never replace Jesus's presence with a fallible human figure. In Jesus's name, amen.*

—Angela N. Parker

35. Fringe Benefits

Luke 20:45-47

"They devour widows' houses and for the sake of appearance say long prayers." (Luke 20:47)

Paula White, Creflo Dollar, and other "prosperity gospel" preachers are easy targets for our derision. Their extravagant lifestyles contradict Christianity's basic teachings. They pray lengthy prayers and talk piously, but their fancy robes and material excess are funded by their followers, who often face financial struggle. We find solace in Luke's promise that God judges such exploitations by religious leaders.

Indeed, the way religious leaders of his time took advantage of the vulnerable instead of coming to their rescue is a constant thread throughout Jesus's ministry. Enjoying a privileged social status and operating corruptly in service to the Roman Empire, these leaders were castigated for straying far from the purposes of God. Rather than aid the widows who were socially and economically disadvantaged in a patriarchal society, the male religious leaders funded their lavish ways by preying upon women in distress.

While I'm not in the habit of defending televangelists, casting them in the mold of Jesus's opponents ignores our own complicity in the plight of the economically vulnerable. In our consumerist society, spending drives the economy, and wages often fail to cover basic needs. Many Americans live paycheck to paycheck.

We may not live like Joel Osteen, but those of us with retirement funds, pensions, and brokerage accounts reap the benefit of this economic structure as stock prices rise from people earning too little and spending too much. Undoubtedly, the harsh words of Jesus apply to others, but we should not deny how they also condemn us.

Prayer: *God, extend your mercy to those of us who benefit from the unjust structures of our world. Allow us to see our complicity, so that our sense of moral urgency to transform them would increase and our pious words would not ring hollow. Contritely we pray, amen.*

—Beau Underwood

36. King of Kings

John 18:33-37
"'You are a king, then!' said Pilate.
Jesus answered, 'You say that I am a king. In fact, the reason I was
born and came into the world is to testify to the truth. Everyone on
the side of truth listens to me.'" (John 18:37)

In checkers, a literal game-changing moment occurs whenever one piece makes it to the opposite end of the board. Growing up, my friends and I would proudly say, "King me" at that time. The newly kinged piece gained fresh powers, as it could travel in any direction to start hunting down pieces of the opposite color. The arrival of a king changed the game.

Those of us in the U.S. don't appreciate the power of a king. We can openly criticize our President and even vote out the person. Challenging authority is our national birthright.

But in Jesus's day, democratic freedoms didn't exist. Challenging the rule of the king (or Caesar or Pharaoh) could gain one a quick ticket to the next life. Rulers often didn't sit quitely as some usurper claimed the title.

So many of the ways we describe Jesus actually presented an accusing challenge to Caesar and his appointed minions like PIlate. Words that we often spiritualize, like "Lord" and "Savior" and even "son of God," instead described Caesar's political power. As did words like "gospel." So, it's no wonder Pilate found Jesus's talk about being a "king" with a "kingdom" so important.

Once we read the Bible with an eye on the political understandings of those words, we start to see the inevitable clash to come. Jesus would either sit on the throne in Jerusalem or die on a cross just outside the city. There is no middle ground for kings.

Prayer: King Jesus, thank you for offering a different way to the selfish rule of kings and dictators. Help me to understand the political implications of your words still today. Help me to remember I can only serve one master—and I want it to be you.

—Brian Kaylor

37. Are You A Chaplain for the Empire or a Prophet for Transformation?

John 19:1-16

"They cried out, 'Away with him! Away with him! Crucify him!' Pilate asked them, 'Shall I crucify your King?' The chief priests answered, 'We have no king but the emperor.'" (John 19:15)

I have always been fascinated by this particular passage of scripture wherein Pilate seemingly gets the chief priests to admit that the emperor is their king even over the God of Abraham, Isaac, and David. In this particular moment of scripture, the chief priests act as chaplains for the empire since they seek to crucify Jesus in order to retain their own positions of power and good standing with the Roman Empire.

Prior to our focus text, Jesus says to Pilate that he would not have any power over Jesus unless it had been given to him from above. Jesus, as the prophet for transformation, knows that power over him (and his followers) does not come from the imperial authorities who think they are in control. Nay, power comes from God above. Contra the chaplains for the empire, as prophets for transformation of social injustices into social justice, we must follow the example of Jesus and strongly speak the truth about authority and to the authorities so that we can be agents of social transformation.

Prayer: *To the God of transformation, please place in our hearts the ability to claim the authority that God has given to us as we embark on social transformation. In Jesus's name, Amen.*

—Angela N. Parker

38. Insurrection

Mark 15:1-7

"Now it was the custom at the festival to release a prisoner whom the people requested. A man called Barabbas was in prison with the insurrectionists who had committed murder in the uprising." (Mark 15:6-7)

Our English translations of the Bible sometimes mislead us as we read the texts about Jesus's crucifixion. Many versions describe him as crucified between "two thieves." But that's not a good translation of the Greek word (*lēstai*), nor does it match with the historical account of Roman crucifixion. We should instead think of them as insurrectionists.

The newest version of the NIV captures this by calling them "rebels." The New Living Translation uses "revolutionaries." And the Romans were fond of crucifying would-be messiahs and their bands of rebels trying to overthrow imperial rule.

We might picture this text today as something like the FBI snatching up a meddling preacher who overturned tables in the gift shop of the National Cathedral and then crucifying him on a hillside outside Washington, D.C., with two Proud Boys arrested for breaking into the Capitol during the deadly insurrection of January 6, 2021.[11]

This impacts our reading of the story. If Jesus is crucified with two thieves, we focus on his innocence since we know he's not a robber. But if Jesus is crucified between two rebels in the place of the leader of the insurrection (Barabbas) with a political declaration that he's the "king of the Jews" (a title only Rome could bestow), we start to realize why Rome killed him. They saw Jesus's message as a revolutionary threat to their rule. But instead we try to domesticate him behind what Martin Luther King Jr. called "the anesthetizing security of stained-glass windows."[12]

Prayer: *Revolutionary God, help me to see the power of your kingdom to disrupt the ways of this world. May I be part of this peaceful overturning of injustice and corruption. And help me to see this story with fresh eyes so I may better follow you.*

—Brian Kaylor

[11]For a longer version of this modern retelling, see: Brian Kaylor, "Crucified between two Proud Boys," *Word&Way*, March 31, 2021, https://wordandway.org/2021/03/31/crucified-between-two-proud-boys/

[12]Martin Luther King Jr., "Letter from a Birmingham Jail," April 16, 1963, https://www.africa.upenn.edu/Articles_Gen/Letter_Birmingham.html

39. Prelude to Resurrection

John 11:17-27

"Jesus said to her, 'I am the resurrection and the life. Those who believe in me, even though they die, will live, and everyone who lives and believes in me will never die.'" (John 11:25-26)

Once the prelude started, it was time to be quiet. That was the expectation in the church where I grew up (and in several churches I've participated in since). The music indicated a shift in time and focus. Our attention turned away from the busyness of our lives to focus on a new encounter with God as worship began.

The raising of Lazarus operates in a similar way. The transition from Jesus's teaching and public ministry to his death and resurrection would be too abrupt. We need a moment to recenter ourselves and prepare for what's about to happen.

In the performing of this miracle, we learn something about Jesus's identity as Messiah. He offers hope despite the reality of death. In Jesus, we find resurrection and life.

That's good news, given the tribulations we encounter. All of us know the agony of Martha. We find ourselves angry at death's intrusion. We share the outrage at God for not preventing its arrival.

Later in John 11, Jesus fulfills his promise by raising Lazarus from the dead. But he is not immortal. He will die again. Like other stories in the gospels, the meaning of the miracle is more important than the act itself. Only the Son of God can raise the dead.

At a time when human rulers claimed divine power and threatened human life, Jesus's raising of Lazaraus is a prelude to the confrontation of the cross. Our faith must be placed not in those with the power to kill, but in the One who can bring life.

Prayer: God of Life, death is all around us. It pretends to be the ultimate power in the world. Do not let it fool us. Keep our faith in the resurrection and the life strong, even when the sting of death arises. In Jesus's name we pray, amen.

—Beau Underwood

40. Hosanna!

Luke 19:36-44

"Blessed is the king who comes in the name of the Lord! Peace in heaven and glory in the highest!" (Luke 19:38)

On Palm Sunday, the children of my church join with kids from another downtown congregation to march along the sidewalk while waving palm leaves. And a donkey goes with them, so that makes it fun for children—especially when it poops (something young boys like my son particularly giggle about).

The first time my son joined this parade during the Sunday School hour, I went along as one of the adults making sure no one got run over. (I wonder which disciple had the job of crowd control back then.)

But the part that stood out for me wasn't the donkey or its offerings. We live in a state capital. In fact, the Governor's Mansion is just a block from our church, and the Capitol building lies another half-block farther. So, as I walked along, I wondered if this is what it might look like to understand that event today.

Was ol' Governor Pilate peeking out the window of the Mansion as the children walked by while waving their palms leaves and shouting "Hosanna!" to honor a different ruler? That first Palm Sunday wasn't an innocent spiritual declaration. People rallying to welcome a would-be deliverer would concern the person they needed delivering from—Rome's own puppet ruler.

But unlike earlier in the gospels, Jesus doesn't try to stop the crowds. This time he says the stones will cry out if he doesn't. The time for his kingdom is nearing. And that should scare a little ruler like Pilate.

Prayer: *Almighty King, may my life shout out hosannas for you—not just today in church but each day out in the streets as well. I don't want a stone to take my place. And as I lift you up, help me not to trust in false messiahs.*

—Brian Kaylor

41. Ready to Be Foolish

1 Corinthians 1:18
For the message of the cross is foolishness to those who are perishing, but to us who are being saved it is the power of God. (1 Corinthians 1:18)

Alice Walker states that to avoid the appearance of foolishness, people actually remain fools. The Apostle Paul writes in 1 Corinthians 1 that the message of the cross is foolish for many. Further, he writes that the Corinthian congregation must consider their own calls as they ponder the foolishness of God.

As we begin to bring our Lenten journey to a close, by the end of this week, we will be meditating at the foot of the cross. Is Christ's cross still foolish today? Can we actually live into the foolishness of Christ while making social transformation today? Is our call to remain judgmental, overbearing Christians who hoard our salvation and our faith over other people? Or are we called to walk with humanity in a way that we model the foolishness of Christ's love with other people?

The last question reminds me of a quotation from Cole Arthur Riley. She writes, "[When] we force our picture of God on another, or when God is presented as singular, we tend to colonize the image of God in others."[13] I am actually ready to be foolish and allow God to be God for myself and other people in whatever way God shows up. This may be foolishness to some, but I think it's beneficial to all. Are you ready to be foolish with me?

Prayer: Most gracious and wise God, we do not know all the answers nor the right questions to ask. Even still, allow us to be a part of your foolishness-making in the world so that others can experience your love and grace.

—Angela N. Parker

---

[13]Cole Arthur Riley, *This Here Flesh*, (Convergent Press), 7.

42. Are You Ready?

Matthew 21:18-22

"Jesus answered them, 'Truly I tell you, if you have faith and do not doubt, not only will you do what has been done to the fig tree, but even if you say to this mountain, 'Be lifted up and thrown into the sea,' it will be done.'" (Matthew 21:21)

The playlist of music I listen to at the gym could be alternatively described as "authentic" or "embarrassing." At risk of dating myself, I admit that one of my favorite songs on there is Creed's "Are You Ready?" The lyrics focus my attention on why—even entering middle age—I continue to physically challenge my body: I'm getting ready for the opportunities and challenges yet to come.

Nearing his death and resurrection, Jesus oddly curses a fig tree to teach his disciples a similar lesson. His life and ministry are nearing an end, but what God is doing through him is just beginning. Indeed, what appears to give life (the fig tree) may ultimately end up barren, and what seems impossible (moving mountains) can happen because the world is being turned upside down through Christ.

Breaking out of our usual expectations to see Lent in fresh ways has been a major emphasis of this devotional. Approaching this holy season the same way each year results in us taking away the same lessons. Unsettling our assumptions creates fertile soil for spiritual growth.

Our preparation intensifies during Holy Week. The narrative of the gospels quickens as the plot nears its climax. What are you still holding onto that might prevent you from arriving in the upper room, gathering at the cross, sitting in grief, or experiencing the empty tomb in new ways? What presumptions still linger?

The old has to pass away for the new to come (2 Corinthians 5:17). Are you ready?

Prayer: *Holy One, you are the God who makes all things new. Unsettle our expectations so that we move through this holiest of weeks open to new possibilities. Where mountains stand in the way of your desires for us and our world, O God, grant us a faith that believes they can—and will—be moved. Through the power of Jesus's name, amen.*

—Beau Underwood

43. Judas Today

Matthew 26:14-16

Then one of the Twelve—the one called Judas Iscariot—went to the chief priests and asked, 'What are you willing to give me if I deliver him over to you?'" (Matthew 26:14-15)

In 2021, prosecutors arrested Judas for participating in the January 6, 2021, insurrection. Okay, it wasn't the biblical Judas, but the Justice Department did arrest an actor playing Judas in *Jesus Christ Superstar*.

"I'd sell out the nation," Judas declares in the play, life imitating art.

The actor got into his part. Before his arrest, *Equality 365* asked him about playing Judas amid "the current social unrest" since "part of the story of Jesus is about rebellion against authority."[14]

"I don't look at it as Judas being a bad guy. I think he is a hero," he answered. "However that is translated into today's society, I hope it would be looked on as a good thing. Tim Rice asks, 'What did Judas do in these times?'"

What would Judas do in these times? Storming the Capitol isn't a bad answer. The chants of "We want Trump!" echoed those two thousand years earlier for Barrabas.

The real Judas felt remorse and killed himself before the mob rooted for Barabbas, but perhaps his betrayal came as he realized Jesus wouldn't bring about the expected messianic overthrow of the Romans. Even in the play, Judas misses the point; the voice of the deceased disciple says, "If you'd come today, you could have reached a whole nation. Israel in 4 B.C. had no mass communication."

Even if Jesus came today, we'd still execute him. MAGAchurches would sell him for some silver while cheering for insurrectionists. Some would even play the part of Judas.

Prayer: *God of all, help me to learn from the fall of Judas and keep me from the temptation to sell out your way for another. Help me follow your kingdom above all others, even when I doubt you. And when I stumble, help me find you again.*

—Brian Kaylor

---

[14]Eric Andrews-Katz, "Interview: James T. Justis—What would Judas Do?," *Equality 365*, Oct. 5, 2021, https://equality365.com/interview-james-t-justis-what-would-judas-do/

44. His (Almost) Final Act

John 13:1-9

"Jesus knew that his hour had come to depart from this world...
Then he poured water into a basin and began to wash the disciples'
feet." (John 13:1,5)

If you knew your life was coming to an end, how would you spend your last days? From Tolstoy's *The Death of Ivan Ilyich* to the 2007 movie *The Bucket List*, a lot of culture and human reflection has been inspired by that question.

A common thread is an intense focus on one's self. The limited time available creates a sense of urgency to mend relationships, enjoy experiences, and fulfill unmet desires. Making the most of the closing window is one more exercise in individualism.

Aware of his looming death, Jesus takes a remarkably different path in his final hours. He washes the feet of his disciples, even Judas. Taking the form of a servant, he humbly performs a task typically reserved for those society respects the least. This act is so unseemly that Peter vigorously objects to Jesus's insistence.

Peter's protest is more familiar than it might seem. A lot of energy is invested in reinforcing a social order that values some more than others. Anger stirs an outcry whenever church and political prophets try to alter the balance of power. After all, "that's just how things are done."

Of course, we are all mortal creatures. Like Jesus, every one of us is headed towards death. That means we face a stark choice. Do we use our limited time on this earth focused on our own selves, or are we devoted to serving others in the most scandalous of ways?

***Prayer:** Self-emptying God, in Jesus Christ you gave all of yourself to the world. This act of humility allowed us to enter into a new relationship with you. Like Jesus, may we be inspired by your love to willingly lower ourselves in order to help raise others up. In his glorious name we pray, amen.*

—Beau Underwood

45. Sometimes You Have To Break the System

Mark 14:1-9
"While he was at Bethany in the house of Simon the leper, as he sat at the table, a woman came with an alabaster jar of very costly ointment of nard, and she broke open the jar and poured the ointment on his head." (Mark 14:3)

Recently, I was watching the ABC miniseries *Women of the Movement*, which depicts events surrounding Emmett Till's murder in 1955. Fourteen-year-old Till was visiting relatives in Money, Mississippi, when he was murdered by two White men for supposedly whistling at a White woman. Seeking to put the matter away quietly, officials buried Till's body without the consent of his mother, Mamie Till-Mobley. Till-Mobley fought hard to have her son's body exhumed and transported to Chicago for a proper burial. After viewing her child's broken body, Till-Mobley "broke" the system of "keeping it quiet" by having an open casket funeral so that the nation had to wrestle with what grown men did to her child.

The story of the anointing woman also "breaks" the system. In Mark 14:1-2, the chief priests conspire to seize Jesus in order to kill him. Transitioning to a house in Bethany, we find an unnamed woman about to anoint Jesus. Jesus is reclining at table, the uninvited woman approaches from behind bearing an alabaster jar of perfume, pure and costly, and then suddenly at 14:3, breaking the alabaster (*suntripsasa ten alabastron*), she pours it on his head.

The Greek verb *suntripso* has a range of meanings. In the context of Mark 14:3, the verb means to smash, crush, or shatter into pieces. In other contexts, such as in Romans 16:20, the verb means to overcome one's enemies. Referring to an emotional state of mind, the verb means to deprive someone of strength as in Luke 4:18. The only other time that the Markan narrative uses the verb is in Mark 5:4 as it describes the Gerasene demoniac breaking his shackles into pieces.

Juxtaposing the scenario between Mamie Till-Mobley and the anointing woman, I argue that both women demonstrate a "breaking" that acts as consciousness raising in the contexts in which they find themselves. The anointing woman understands that Jesus's body is about to undergo destruction at the hands of Roman imperial violence. Mamie Till-Mobley demanded that the nation view White supremacist violence effected upon her child. Both women broke some systems in order to bring understanding.

Prayer: *Gracious God, sometimes we are comfortable in systems that privilege us. Please give us the gumption to break systems that oppress ourselves and other people. Amen.*

—Angela N. Parker

46. V for Victory?

Matthew 27:62-66

"'Take a guard,' Pilate answered. 'Go, make the tomb as secure as you know how.' So, they went and made the tomb secure by putting a seal on the stone and posting the guard.'" (Matthew 27:65-66)

Richard Nixon refused to accept victory. Having lost the presidency in 1960 by the second-closest margin in history and then losing the 1962 California gubernatorial contest, paranoia took over as his presidential reelection campaign neared in 1972.

He didn't need to worry. He would win a blowout, painting forty-eight states red. But he managed to snatch defeat from the jaws of victory. Despite advantages in incumbency, financing, and polling, he saw enemies behind every shadow. He and his team wouldn't leave the election to fate or even the voters. So, they broke into the Democratic headquarters in the Watergate hotel.

The ironic thing is that he didn't need to cheat. But the scandal and coverup drove him from office in shame like Adam and Eve. Rather than winning him more time in the White House, it sent him packing as he still flashed his famous *V* signs for some victory that would never again come.

We see the same paranoia after the state execution of Jesus. Unable to accept victory, they continued plotting. The intoxication of power sends us consuming shot after shot even as the world spins and reality blurs.

That religious and political leaders still feared Jesus even after they lynched him reveals their feelings of impotence from just hearing his name. Refusing to let him rest in peace, they demonstrated the injustice of their leadership.

But in this case their schemes are for naught. You can't outwit the King of kings nor guard against the lion of Judah.

Prayer: Conqueror of death, help me to trust in you even on those dark days like that Saturday when it seems evil has won. Even if victory doesn't come the next day, may I not join the efforts to trample justice and discard peace.

—Brian Kaylor

47. Sunday's Not Here Yet

John 19:38-42

"Because it was the Jewish day of Preparation and since the tomb was nearby, they laid Jesus there." (John 19:42)

Some churches celebrate "Easter Vigil" late on Saturday night or in the wee hours of Sunday. It's not quite Resurrection Day yet. So, we pause for a second time on this dark day between Good Friday and Easter.

It seems good for us to linger here a bit longer. Because we like to jump right to triumphalism. We skip past the pain and lament straight to the celebration. Just look at how little our society paused to lament during the COVID-19 pandemic even as more than six million people globally died in just a couple years.

Tony Campolo likes to tell a story of a "preach off" where he learned five powerful words: "It's Friday, but Sunday's comin'!" While I've learned much from Campolo, I'm not sure this is always a helpful attitude. Sometimes we need to stop on Saturday in the shadow of death.

If the first disciples kept vigil that night it wasn't out of anticipation of resurrection but pure fright. One whispers, "What was that noise? A rodent? A soldier?" But mostly they wondered how he could be dead. The story wasn't supposed to end like this.

"Where are you, God?" another disciple exhales, half in sincere prayer and half in profane disbelief.

Where are you, God, when a deadly virus ripped through our communities—especially in superspreader events on Sunday mornings as churches sang the same old happy songs like nothing is wrong? Where are you, God, as political violence and racist anger poisons our body politic? Where are you, God?

Tonight, we do not celebrate. We mourn and sit in silence for an answer that doesn't seem forthcoming.

Prayer. *Where are you, God? I ask again, hoping for an answer even when I don't expect it. I believe, help me in my unbelief. Where are you, God?*

—Brian Kaylor

48. Time to Shake Things Up!

Matthew 28:1-10

"And suddenly there was a great earthquake; for an angel of the Lord, descending from heaven, came and rolled back the stone and sat on it." (Matthew 28:2)

Bringing our Lenten journey to a close, we all face the question, "What do I do now?" I think we need to shake things up. In the resurrection narrative, the writer states that Mary Magdalene and the other Mary went to see the tomb. As they approach, there was a great earthquake. The Greek word for earthquake is *seismos*. One can understand *seismos* as a great shaking or agitation of the earth.

Similarly, the Matthean writer states that the guards also shook and became like dead men. The writer plays with language that uses the verbal form of *seismos*, the Greek word *seio*, in order to connect the earthquake on the ground with the shaking of the people. There comes a time in our Christian walk where we have to shake both the earth and the people!

As a Christian and as a Black woman, I have taken part in #BlackLivesMatter movements. The BLM movement coalesced under the leadership of Patrisse Cullors, Opal Tometi, and Alicia Garza after the murder of Trayvon Martin on February 26, 2012. The movement began a roar, but the murder of George Floyd was the beginning of the earthquake. On May 31, 2020, Floyd was murdered by a White Minneapolis police officer who knelt on Floyd's neck for nine minutes and twenty-nine seconds. After the nonchalant murder was caught on cellphone video, people around the globe witnessed the murder, and subsequent protests erupted around the globe.

As we remember and celebrate the ministry, death, and resurrection of Jesus Christ, we must tend to the unfinished business of securing God's reign and peace on the earth. A shaking must occur. Let us shake the world!

Prayer: Heavenly God, allow us to remember that as Christians, we must strive to be the hands and feet of God here on Earth as we shake the world to be a socially just society.

—Angela N. Parker